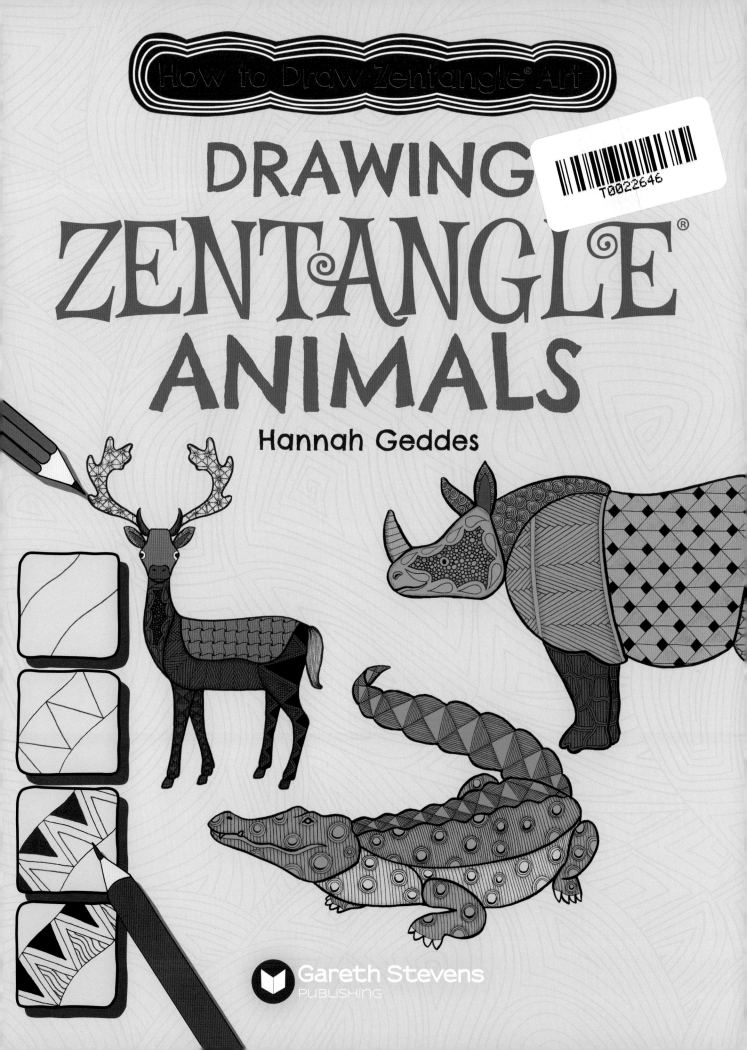

How to Draw Zentangle® Art

DRAWING
ZENTANGLE®
ANIMALS

Hannah Geddes

Gareth Stevens
PUBLISHING

Acknowledgments

The Zentangle® method was created by Rick Roberts and Maria Thomas.

"Zentangle"®, the Zentangle® logo, "Anything is possible one stroke at a time", "Bijou", "Certified Zentangle Teacher"®, "CZT"®, "Zentangle Apprentice"®, and "Zentomology" are trademarks, service marks, or certification marks of Rick Roberts, Maria Thomas, and/or Zentangle Inc.

PERMISSION TO COPY ARTWORKS: The written instructions, designs, patterns, and projects in this book are intended for the personal use of the reader and may be reproduced for that purpose only. Any other use, especially commercial use, is forbidden under law without the written permission of the copyright holder.

All the tangles in this book are Zentangle® originals created by Rick Roberts and Maria Thomas, apart from: Vache 1 (page 17) and Wartz (page 12) by Genevieve Crabe CZT.

Please visit our website, www.garethstevens.com.
For a free color catalog of all our high-quality books,
call toll free 1-800-542-2595 or fax 1-877-542-2596.

CATALOGING-IN-PUBLICATION DATA

Names: Geddes, Hannah.
Title: Drawing Zentangle® animals / Hannah Geddes.
Description: New York : Gareth Stevens Publishing, 2018. | Series: How to draw Zentangle® art | Includes index.
Identifiers: ISBN 9781538207208 (pbk.) | ISBN 9781538207154 (library bound) | ISBN 9781538207055 (6 pack)
Subjects: LCSH: Drawing--Technique--Juvenile literature. | Repetitive patterns (Decorative arts)--Juvenile literature. | Animals in art--Juvenile literature.
Classification: LCC NC730.G43 2018 | DDC 741.201'9--dc23

Published in 2018 by
Gareth Stevens Publishing
111 East 14th Street, Suite 349
New York, NY 10003

Copyright © 2018 Arcturus Holdings Limited

Step-outs and Zentangle® Inspired Artworks by Hannah Geddes
Text by Catherine Ard
Outline illustrations by Katy Jackson
Designed by Trudi Webb and Emma Randall
Edited by Frances Evans

Printed in China
CPSIA compliance information: Batch CS17GS: For further information contact
Gareth Stevens, New York, New York at 1-800-542-2595.

Contents

Animal Magic

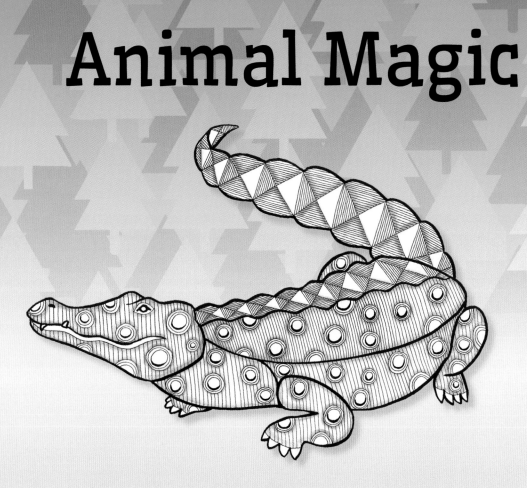

Zentangle® is a drawing method created by Rick Roberts and Maria Thomas. It teaches you how to create beautiful pieces of art using simple **patterns** called tangles. Tangling is a really fun, relaxing way to get creative, and it brings out the artist in everyone. You can tangle wherever and whenever the mood takes you!

The animal kingdom is a great place to look for artwork inspiration. This book uses the wonder of wildlife to show you how to create Zentangle® Inspired Artworks ("ZIAs"). You'll learn animal-inspired tangles that can be used to decorate anything from a gentle rhinoceros to a playful squirrel.

Pens and Pencils

Pencils are good for drawing "strings" (page 18) and for adding shade to your tangles. A 01 (0.25-mm) black pen is good for fine lines. Use a 05 (0.45-mm) or 08 (0.50-mm) pen to fill in bigger areas. You can use paints to brighten up your art, too!

Paper

Tangles are usually drawn on a square 3.5-inch (9 cm) tile made of thin cardboard. You can use any kind of paper, but if you want to make your tangles really special, use good quality art paper. Have some tracing paper on hand so you can trace the images in this book to use as outlines for your Zentangle® Inspired Artworks.

Useful Techniques

There are some special techniques you might come across when you tangle. A "highlight" is a gap or blank space in the lines of your tangles. Highlights can make your tangles look shiny!

An "aura" is a line traced around the inside or outside of a shape. Use auras to add a sense of movement to your art.

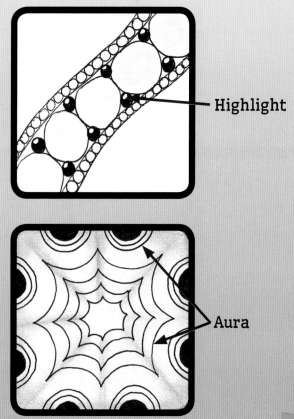

Highlight

Aura

Essential Tangles

Here are some fantastic tangles to get you started! You can practice drawing each tangle on a square tile (see step 1 on page 18 for instructions). Each project in this book has a tangle key that tells you where to find the instructions for the tangles that have been used.

Tipple

1. Start by drawing a small circle on your paper.

2. Add a few more circles around the first one. They can be any size you like.

3. Keep drawing circles of different sizes until the chosen space is full.

4. Shade in the spaces between the circles to finish your tangle.

Bales

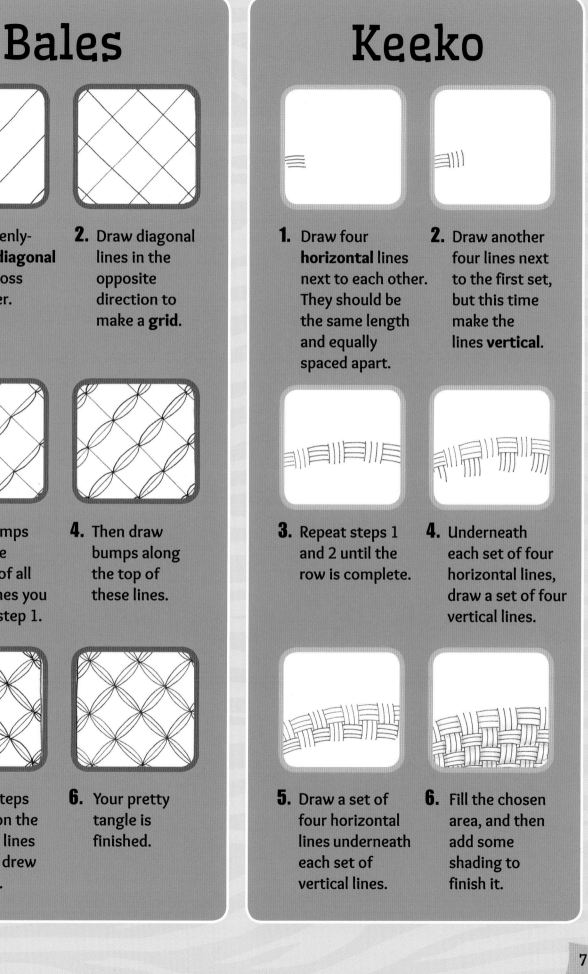

1. Draw evenly-spaced **diagonal** lines across the paper.

2. Draw diagonal lines in the opposite direction to make a **grid**.

3. Draw bumps along the bottom of all of the lines you drew in step 1.

4. Then draw bumps along the top of these lines.

5. Repeat steps 3 and 4 on the diagonal lines that you drew in step 2.

6. Your pretty tangle is finished.

Keeko

1. Draw four **horizontal** lines next to each other. They should be the same length and equally spaced apart.

2. Draw another four lines next to the first set, but this time make the lines **vertical**.

3. Repeat steps 1 and 2 until the row is complete.

4. Underneath each set of four horizontal lines, draw a set of four vertical lines.

5. Draw a set of four horizontal lines underneath each set of vertical lines.

6. Fill the chosen area, and then add some shading to finish it.

Cadent

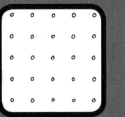 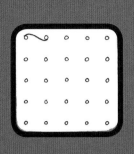 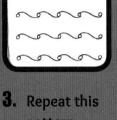  

1. Draw a grid made up of small circles.

2. Draw a curve from the top of the first circle to the bottom of the second circle.

3. Repeat this pattern across each horizontal row of circles.

4. Now, use the same pattern to join up the vertical lines of circles.

5. Your Cadent tangle is complete.

'Nzeppel

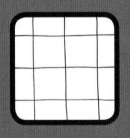 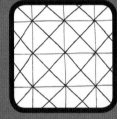   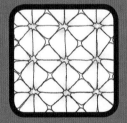

1. Draw horizontal and vertical lines over the paper to make a grid.

2. Now draw diagonal lines in both directions over the paper. They should be evenly spaced so they run through the middle of each square in the grid.

3. Each square in the grid should now be split into four triangular sections. Draw around the shape of each triangle, but round off the corners to create this pebble-like effect.

4. Continue to fill each square with triangles, as shown.

5. Add some shading to finish your tangle.

Printemps

This tangle is perfect for creating swirly textures.

1. Draw a dot in the middle of your page. Then begin to draw a small **spiral** starting from the dot.

2. Continue drawing your spiral. You can make it as small or as big as you like.

3. Once the spiral is the size that you want, turn the line in to close up the shape. You should have a smooth circle around the edge.

4. Add more spiral shapes around the first one.

5. Continue drawing Printemps spirals until you have filled the space.

Diva Dance

This wavy, bumpy tangle works well
for anything that is on the move.

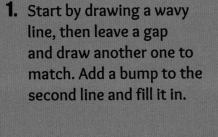

1. Start by drawing a wavy line, then leave a gap and draw another one to match. Add a bump to the second line and fill it in.

2. Draw another pair of lines that flow around the bump. Keep the lines evenly spaced apart. Add another bump on a different part of the second line and fill it in.

3. Continue this pattern, adding pairs of lines with a bump somewhere along the second line.

4. Make some bumps longer, some shorter, and some wider so that your tangle has a natural look.

Knase

This spiky tangle will give any picture an edge.

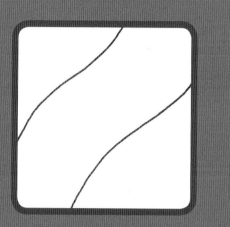

1. Start by drawing two evenly-spaced diagonal lines.

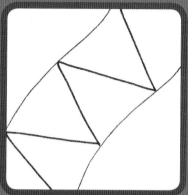

2. Draw a zigzag between the two lines.

3. Draw triangles inside the top row of the zigzag and fill them in. Now draw triangles inside the bottom row of the zigzag.

4. Finally, fill each triangle in the bottom row with wavy lines.

5. Your tangle is complete!

Tangle Tip!
The zigzags in Knase would be perfect for a tiger or zebra picture!

Wartz

Stripes **contrast** with the circles on this tangle to create a bold, bumpy **texture**.

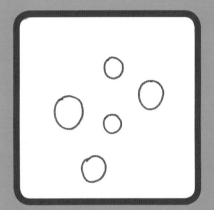

1. Draw a group of different-sized circles in the middle of the page. Keep the circles close to each other.

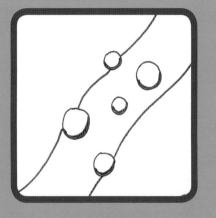

2. Add a thick line at the bottom of each circle. Now add two wavy lines going across the middle of the page. When you reach a circle, stop the line and then continue it on the other side.

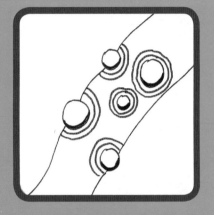

3. Draw two auras around each circle. When a circle overlaps a line, only draw the aura around the part that is inside the line.

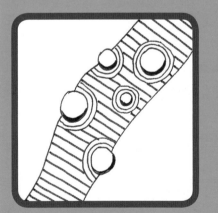

4. Draw stripes to fill the area inside the wavy lines. Stop the lines at the edge of each aura.

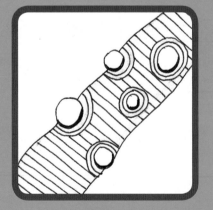

5. Your tangle is ready. You could shade along the edges of the wavy lines and around the circles to make them stand out.

Tangle Tip!
This knobbly tangle would be perfect for a toad picture. You could use it to create a tree bark texture, too.

Avreal

The strong shapes and sharp edges in this tangle are perfect for spikes and spines.

1. Start by drawing two pairs of slightly curved lines with a space in between, like this.

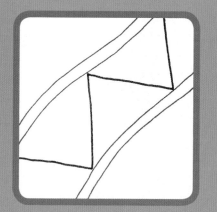

2. Draw a zigzag between the pairs of lines.

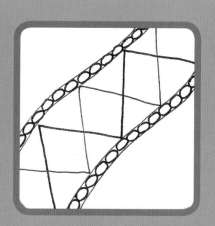

3. Draw another zigzag line from the opposite side to make a row of diamonds. Fill the areas between the pairs of lines with ovals.

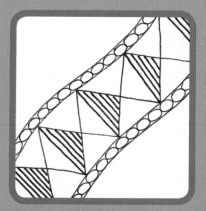

4. Fill the right half of each diamond with straight lines.

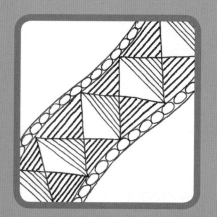

5. Then add horizontal lines above and below the diamonds. When you reach a diamond, stop the line and then continue it on the other side.

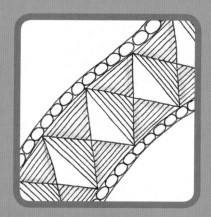

6. Add shading to finish your tangle.

Ennies

Try this pretty tangle of pebbles framed with petals for a natural touch.

1. Draw a petal shape lying on its side at the bottom of the space.

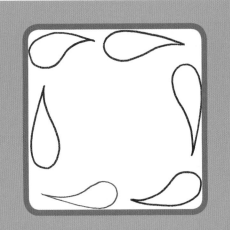

2. Add more petal shapes around the outside.

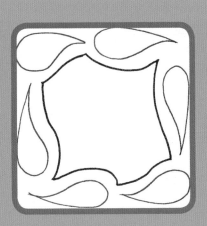

3. Draw an inner frame, following the outlines of the petals.

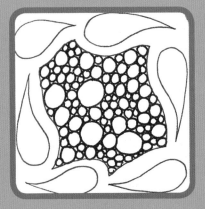

4. Add lots of closely-packed circles inside the frame, making them all different sizes.

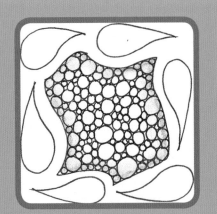

5. Shade along the inside edges of the frame with a pencil and smudge with your finger to finish.

Tangle Tip!

The tightly packed circles and loose petal frame create a nice contrast. Use this tangle on parts of your picture that you want to stand out!

Hibred

Weave some magic into your artwork with this tidy, criss-cross tangle.

1. Draw two pairs of lines with a space in between, like this.

2. Draw a zigzag between the pairs of lines.

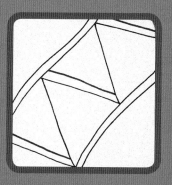

3. Add a line inside each "V" of the zigzag, starting on the left.

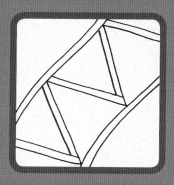

4. Now, add a line inside each "V" on the right.

5. Continue to add lines, first on the left, then on the right, to fill the space.

6. Now start to add upside down "Vs" in the empty triangles, starting on the right.

7. Now add a line on the left. Continue adding lines on the right and then the left until the space is filled.

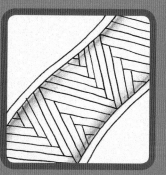

8. Shade along the edges with a pencil and smudge it with your finger.

Cubine

Check out the squares on this tangle! It's perfect for giving large areas a bold look.

1. Draw evenly-spaced diagonal lines from left to right across the paper.

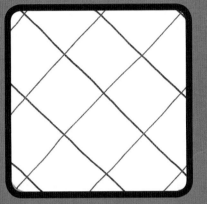

2. Now add diagonal lines going in the opposite direction.

3. Draw a small box in the right-hand corner of each square and fill it in.

4. Add a line from the left-hand corner of each square to the right-hand corner of each box.

5. Shade above the line in each square to finish your tangle.

Tangle Tip!
Try changing the size of the grid to create a different look. You could experiment with vertical or curved lines, too!

Vache 1

This patterned tangle creates a texture that is perfect for giraffe's fur or tough rhino skin.

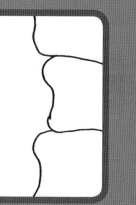

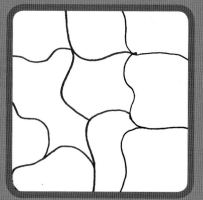

1. Start by drawing loose shapes on your paper. They can be any size or shape you like, but the edges must touch.

2. Draw more shapes until you have filled up the whole area.

3. Inside each shape, draw a smaller shape that follows the same outline.

4. Fill each smaller shape with vertical lines that are evenly spaced apart.

5. Your tangle is complete!

Strings, Tangles, and ZIAs

The Zentangle® method begins with drawing "strings." These are pencil lines that separate spaces inside a shape. The spaces are then filled with tangles to create your ZIA. Each project in this book starts with an outline of an animal with the strings already drawn in.

These steps show you how to build up a set of Zentangle® patterns on a Zentangle® tile. Tiles are good for practicing the tangles you've just learned. They can also be works of art themselves!

1. To create a square tile, use a ruler and pencil to draw four evenly-spaced dots for the corners. Connect the dots with straight lines.

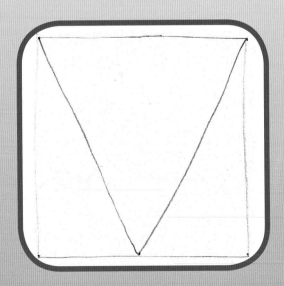

2. Now add strings to divide up the square. Draw a dot in the center of the bottom line. Then draw strings from the top corners to the new dot. This will create three triangle shapes to fill with tangles.

3. Choose a section to fill and a tangle to start with. We've chosen Printemps (page 9). Starting in one corner and using a pen, carefully fill the area with the tangle.

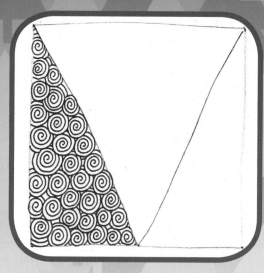

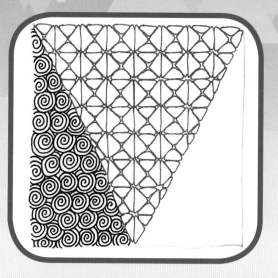

4. Now move to the next space created by the string. We've chosen to fill this section with 'Nzeppel (page 8).

5. In the final space, we've used Bales (page 7).

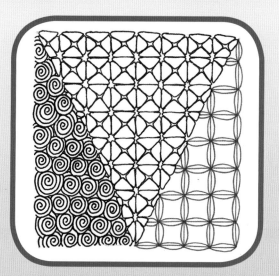

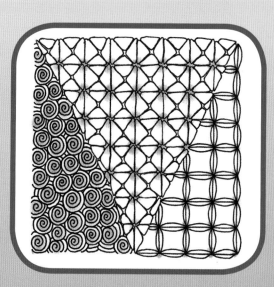

6. To complete the tangles, add shading to create shape and texture.

Now you're ready to start your own tangles!

Stealthy Jaguar

A jaguar's spotty markings keep it hidden as it slinks through the jungle. Follow these steps to create your own big cat with a cool Zentangle® coat.

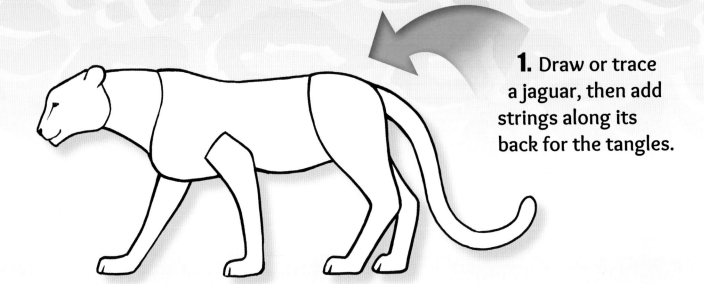

1. Draw or trace a jaguar, then add strings along its back for the tangles.

2. Start to add tangles. We've used Knase for the legs and Printemps for the tail. We've also added some detail to the ear and eye.

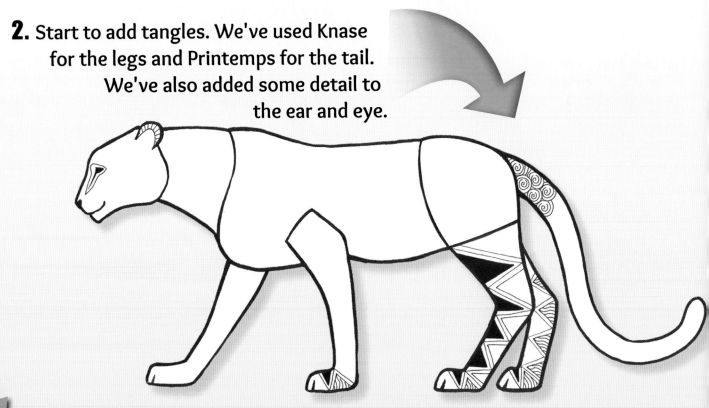

3. Add tangles to the body, section by section. Diva Dance works well here as it shows off the muscular shape of the animal.

TANGLE KEY

Diva Dance: page 10
Knase: page 11
Printemps: page 9

4. Work carefully on the face, making sure the line of the mouth can still be seen.

Snappy Crocodile

Crocodiles like to sunbathe on the banks of muddy rivers. Learn how to create this striking croc with tangles that show off its spiky tail and scaly skin.

1. Carefully copy this crocodile outline. Draw strings along its body for your tangles.

2. Start to fill the spaces between the strings. We've used Avreal on the tail and the top of the back to give a jagged texture.

3. Choose a contrasting tangle for the rest of the crocodile. We've used Wartz on the body and legs to give a scaly look.

TANGLE KEY

Avreal: page 13
Wartz: page 12

4. Draw a line around the eye and below the mouth. Leave these areas untangled when you work on the crocodile's face. We left the claws blank, too.

Playful Squirrel

Squirrels have big, bushy tails to help them balance as they leap through the trees. Follow these steps to create your own cute squirrel with a beautiful tail.

1. Copy this outline of a hungry squirrel. Draw the head, arm, and leg as separate shapes to fill with different tangles and add a string along the body.

2. Start to fill the areas with tangles. We've chosen Bales for the head, Avreal and Knase for the body, and Hibred for the tail.

3. Mix straight line tangles with flowing tangles for a great effect. Here we've used Printemps for the arm, Diva Dance for the leg, 'Nzeppel for the **acorn**, and Keeko for the foot.

4. Add some shading on the tail and body to finish it off.

TANGLE KEY

Avreal: page 13
Bales: page 7
Diva Dance: page 10
Hibred: page 15
Keeko: page 7
Knase: page 11
'Nzeppel: page 8
Printemps: page 9

Stately Stag

Male deer grow a pair of **majestic antlers** every spring.
Follow these simple steps to create your very own
Zentangle®-inspired stag with a beautiful set of antlers!

1. Draw or trace a simple stag outline and add some strings for your tangles.

2. Begin to add some tangles to the outline. We're using Ennies for the neck, Hibred and Cadent for the body, Avreal for the front legs, and Knase for the back legs.

3. Try to pick tangles that contrast with one another. We've chosen 'Nzeppel for the antlers and Printemps for the ears.

TANGLE KEY

Avreal: page 13
Cadent: page 8
Ennies: page 14
Hibred: page 15
Knase: page 11
'Nzeppel: page 8
Printemps: page 9

4. Shade and smudge around the edges of the legs, body, and neck to give your stag a fuller, rounded look.

Gentle Rhino

Rhinos like to keep cool by **wallowing** in muddy **water holes**. Give your rhino a Zentangle® makeover and swap the mud for some amazing tangles!

1. Draw or trace a rhino outline, and add strings where the folds of skin would fall.

2. We've chosen four bold tangles for the main body sections: Hibred, Cubine, Keeko, and 'Nzeppel. We've also added detail to the **horn**.

TANGLE KEY
Cubine: page 16
Ennies: page 14
Hibred: page 15
Keeko: page 7
'Nzeppel: page 8
Printemps: page 9
Vache 1: page 17

3. Pick something with more detail for the head. We've used Ennies for the face and Printemps for the ears and shoulder.

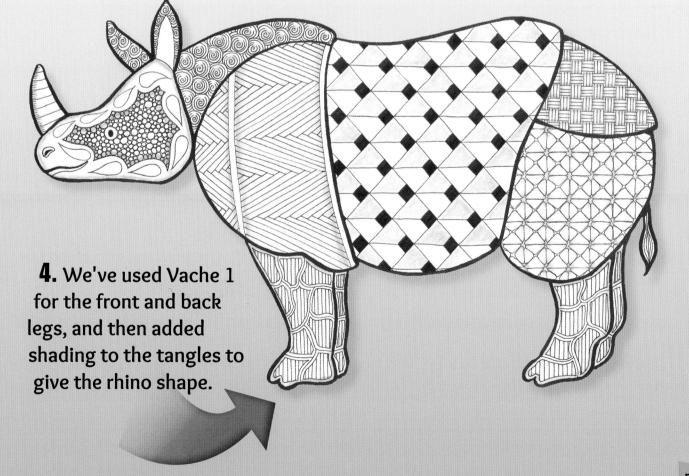

4. We've used Vache 1 for the front and back legs, and then added shading to the tangles to give the rhino shape.

Glossary

acorn The nut or seed of the oak tree.

antler A branched horn that grows from the top of a male deer's head.

contrast To be strikingly different from something else.

diagonal A straight line at an angle.

grid A set of uniform squares made from straight lines or points.

horizontal A straight line that is parallel to the horizon, the imaginary line where the ground meets the sky.

horn A pointed piece of hard bone-like material that grows on the head or face of animals.

majestic Impressive or royal looking.

pattern A set of shapes or a design that is repeated.

spiral A shape made from a line moving outwards in a circular pattern from a central point.

texture The look or feel of a surface.

vertical A line or object that stands straight up, at right angles with the horizon.

wallow To lie or roll in muddy water to keep cool.

water hole A pool of fresh water where animals gather to drink.

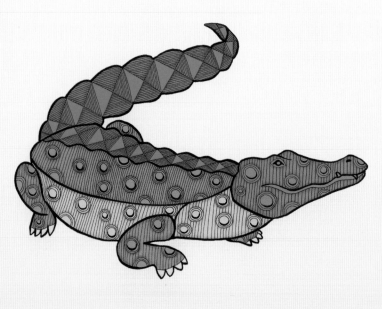

Further Information

Books to Read

Amazing Animal Journeys
Chris Packham
Egmont, 2016

Zentangle® for Kids
by Jane Marbaix
Arcturus Publishing, 2015

Zentangle® for Kids: With Tangles, Templates and Pages to Tangle On
by Beate Winkler
Quarry Books, 2016

Websites

Check out this fun website for coloring pages of marvelous mammals!
www.supercoloring.com/coloring-pages/mammals

Find out more about Zentangle® at the official website.
https://www.zentangle.com

Learn new tangles at this fun site!
http://tanglepatterns.com

Publisher's note to educators and parents: Our editors have carefully reviewed these websites to ensure that they are suitable for students. Many websites change frequently, however, and we cannot guarantee that a site's future contents will continue to meet our high standards of quality and educational value. Be advised that students should be closely supervised whenever they access the Internet.

Index